T0086135

PICKLEBALL

MATCH TRACKER

Trey Sizemore

ADAMS MEDIA

New York   London   Toronto   Sydney   New Delhi

Adams Media
An Imprint of Simon & Schuster, LLC
100 Technology Center Drive
Stoughton, Massachusetts 02072

First Adams Media trade paperback edition April 2024

ADAMS MEDIA and colophon are registered trademarks of Simon & Schuster, LLC.

Simon & Schuster: Celebrating 100 Years of Publishing in 2024

For information about special discounts for bulk purchases, please contact Simon & Schuster Special Sales at 1-866-506-1949 or business@simonandschuster.com.

The Simon & Schuster Speakers Bureau can bring authors to your live event. For more information or to book an event, contact the Simon & Schuster Speakers Bureau at 1-866-248-3049 or visit our website at www.simonspeakers.com.

Interior design by Colleen Cunningham
Interior images © Getty Images/Karelkart, Md Abdul Mannan; 123RF/koblizeek

Manufactured in the United States of America

1 2024

ISBN 978-1-5072-2300-0

Contents

Preface

I first heard about pickleball in 2017. My tennis coach told me he was getting certified to teach pickleball because of the overwhelming number of players taking up the sport. I had no idea what pickleball was, but I thought it would be worth checking out this sport given its skyrocketing popularity and funny name. I started taking some lessons to get a feel for the game. And—probably like you—I was quickly hooked! It was fun, strategic, and easy to start playing.

Even though pickleball was easy to learn, I soon discovered that it was much harder to master. Sure, the court was smaller than the tennis court I was used to, but the two-bounce rule and kitchen added clever twists to the game. It's important to have patience and think one, two, and even three shots ahead. Pickleball was really exciting...and fun!

I had a background in training and enablement (both military and corporate) on a variety of different subjects. I love helping people understand things more comprehensively and quickly. So I began thinking about how I could help players like me get better at pickleball. I wanted to involve some of the top pickleball experts—players and coaches with years of experience who would share their expertise to help players master pickleball more quickly.

And with that, the World Pickleball Summit was born. The World Pickleball Summit, a groundbreaking online event, brought in more than twenty top pickleball players and coaches who generously donated their time to speak with me on a variety of topics that were then shared with pickleball players everywhere. At the same time, I created PickleballHut.com, a resource for pickleball players of all levels to get tips on technique, strategy, mental toughness, and product reviews.

Now I'm putting this knowledge into book form, so you can learn pickleball from the experts! I've included blank forms so you can track your match records, some suggestions for warming up and cooling down, a glossary of common terms, and much more. I'm excited to share this information so you can improve your game too.

Like I tell my students…you've got this!

Trey

P.S. Visit PickleballHut.com/book to find additional tips and information!

Introduction

Fast-paced play.

Simple equipment.

A fun and social environment.

Pickleball really does have it all! Whether you're one of the millions of people already playing pickleball or are just thinking about taking up the sport, *Pickleball: Match Tracker* will help you understand the basic rules and develop your game.

You'll start by learning the brief history of pickleball, then discover the equipment you need and the layout of the court. Once you master some key rules, it's time to start playing.

In addition to getting professional coaching, one of the best things you can do to improve your game is to document and review your progress—and that's where the Match Records section of this book comes in. Use the prompts provided to record your scores, rate different aspects of your play, and capture other key details like weather conditions, match highlights, and challenging plays.

Over time, your notes will reveal patterns that will help you identify your strengths and areas for improvement.

- Which of your skills is your best asset?
- Are particular opponents or playing styles giving you trouble?
- Which of your strokes could use more practice?

Maybe you notice that you often lose to a particular partner because of their strong serve. Or perhaps you struggle on windy days and need to work on playing in challenging outdoor conditions.

Taking just a few minutes after your matches to jot down your thoughts will provide lots of great insights that can take your game to the next level. Use what you learn to highlight your strengths, overcome your weaknesses, and log more wins than ever before.

Whether you're a weekend warrior playing singles matches with a friend or crushing local tournaments with a doubles partner, let *Pickleball: Match Tracker* put the ball in your court and improve your game!

Pickleball 101

It's no wonder pickleball is so popular—it's a fun, social way to exercise. Part Ping-Pong, part tennis, pickleball is affordable, easy to learn, and entertaining for all ages. Whether you're a seasoned player or just taking up the sport, this section will show you all the ins and outs of this dynamic game.

A Brief History of Pickleball

Pickleball has a really interesting origin story. Although it exploded in popularity in the 2020s, it was actually invented in 1965 by Joel Pritchard and Bill Bell, two fathers. On a summer day at Pritchard's house on Bainbridge Island, Washington, the kids wanted to play a game, but all they had were some Ping-Pong paddles, a badminton court, and a plastic ball—not enough equipment for a complete game of anything.

Determined to help their kids entertain themselves, Pritchard and Bell improvised a new game with their existing equipment on the badminton court. The original game was played with the net at badminton height (60 inches), but the plastic ball bounced so well on the asphalt that they lowered the net to 36 inches.

Barney McCallum joined the founding team the next summer. The three men then created a proper court and refined the rules. McCallum was responsible for designing new paddles out of 3/8-inch pieces of plywood made especially for pickleball.

Why Is It Called Pickleball?

There are two competing theories of how the game's name was created. The first comes from Joel Pritchard's wife, Joan. She claimed that the name originated from "pickle boat," a crew boat made up of random rowers, sometimes people who were not chosen to compete on other boats (which calls to mind the mishmash of equipment that pickleball started with). The second (less likely) theory involves the Pritchard family dog, Pickles, who loved to chase after the plastic ball and run off with it.

Many who saw the sport as it was then—neighbors, friends, and acquaintances—eventually asked for their own pickleball equipment. The creators never envisioned pickleball going public, but it was too popular to stay within the three families. The United States Amateur Pickleball Association (USAPA) was formed in 1984, the same year that the first official rulebook was published. The game slowly grew and spread, and in 2009, the first national tournament was held and was attended by over four hundred pickleball fans.

In 2020, USAPA rebranded as USA Pickleball, aligning more closely with other US sports groups. Membership grew in leaps and bounds after the rebranding and media exposure. Today, USA Pickleball estimates that there are about nine million pickleball players over the age of six in the United States, with numerous clubs sprouting up across the world.

The Equipment You Need

Before you take your first steps on the court, you'll need a few items to get started. If you're just beginning, you may want to start with less expensive gear as you determine what suits you best. As you become more experienced, you'll know how to tailor your equipment to make your game more comfortable, competitive, and enjoyable.

Choosing Your Paddle

The paddle is the most important piece of pickleball equipment you'll need. Although the first paddles were wooden (and you can still get wooden paddles), today, most paddles are made of composite materials or graphite. The primary considerations when choosing a paddle are weight, shape, and composition of the surface and core of the paddle.

SURFACE

The outer surface of the paddle will usually be one of the following:

- **Wood:** These are original pickleball paddles. They tend to be the cheapest option and also the heaviest.

- **Composite:** The surfaces of these paddles are usually either fiberglass or carbon fiber. The cores can be aluminum, polymer, or a rigid nylon material called Nomex. These paddles are lighter and tend to be more expensive than wood paddles. This is often the best compromise for beginners taking into account weight, performance, and cost.
- **Graphite:** Graphite paddles have a thin, graphite surface material and similar core options as composite paddles. These paddles are very responsive and lightweight and also tend to be the most expensive.

CORE

The core of the paddle impacts how the ball responds to the paddle. Here are the types of materials used in a paddle's core:

- **Wood:** Paddles with wood cores are usually heavy and dense, which gives your shot more power but also adds extra weight.
- **Aluminum:** This lightweight option tends to sacrifice power/pop on the ball.
- **Polymer:** This material results in a quieter sound than other core materials but provides less power. It's a good option for players who want higher levels of control more than increased power.
- **Nomex:** This material creates a lightweight and highly durable core, though it tends to make the paddle louder than other core materials.

GRIP SIZE

The grip size of the paddle is another factor to consider. If the grip is too big, your paddle might slip, and you may experience elbow problems as a result. Smaller grips allow for more wrist action and thus more control, but some people may grip their paddle too tightly when using smaller grips.

This chart can help you determine what grip size would work best for you. When in doubt, choose the smaller of the sizes.

Player Height	Grip Measurement	Grip Size
Under 5'2"	4"	Small
5'3" to 5'8"	4¼"	Medium
5'9" and taller	4½"	Large

PADDLE SHAPE

Paddles come in a variety of shapes and sizes, but they fall into two main categories: square and elongated.

- The more traditional **square paddles** tend to have a paddle face that is about the same height and width. This makes the paddle a good all-around choice for players—especially beginners—who want to maximize the hitting area in all directions.
- The **elongated paddles** are longer than they are wide and tend to be used during singles matches where the extra reach comes in handy.

Whether square or elongated, the total size of the paddle must fall within the USAPA guidelines. These rules state that the combined length and width, including any edge guard and butt cap, cannot exceed 24 inches. The paddle length cannot exceed 17 inches.

FIND WHAT WORKS FOR YOU

There's no one right paddle for everyone. Try playing with a few different types and determine which one complements your playing style and fits into your budget.

What Should I Wear to Play Pickleball?

Pickleball has a relaxed approach when it comes to what clothing is worn on the court—you will likely prefer lightweight or breathable fabrics since you'll be exercising. Comfort and support are especially important when it comes to choosing your shoes. There's an increasing variety of shoes that are made "specifically for pickleball," but any tennis shoe will be great for outdoor play. If you're particularly aggressive on the court, you may need protective eyewear, arm or leg braces, or gloves to ensure your safety.

Pickleball Balls

You might be surprised to learn that there is no standard pickleball ball. In fact, there are currently dozens of manufacturers that make balls that have been approved by the

USAPA—you can find the full list here: https://equipment.usapickleball.org/ball-list/.

Remember to choose the correct indoor or outdoor balls, though! Indoor balls have fewer, larger holes (approximately twenty-six), compared with outdoor balls (approximately forty holes). More holes make outdoor balls less susceptible to wind (and slightly heavier) and promote faster gameplay.

When you are learning how to play, grab some of the less expensive options. Unlike tennis balls, pickleball balls can last a while, and you'll typically only use one in a match. It won't take long for you to find out which kind you prefer.

Tournament Balls

If you decide to participate in pickleball competitions, it is worth asking what kind of ball the tournament will be using so you can practice with it ahead of time.

Optional Extra Practice Equipment

As the saying goes, practice makes perfect, and that goes for your pickleball game too. Luckily, there are a plethora of tools to make practicing more effective and efficient—and fun! Following is a list of some options you might want to consider to improve your game:

- **Cones:** Placing cones around the court and trying to hit them is a great way to improve your accuracy. These can be used for a number of drills (like your serve or offensive lobs). Cones are especially good for these drills, as they are inexpensive; have bright, distinctive coloring; and don't move easily under normal conditions.

- **Ball machine:** Don't have someone to practice with? No problem. A ball machine is a great way to get consistent feeds, and it will stay on the court with you as long as you want! Ball machines can vary in price considerably and will typically be differentiated by ball capacity, remote control, battery life, ability to add spin, ability to vary directions, A/C adapter, and more. Consider your needs and budget to find one that works for you.
- **Ball hopper/caddy:** When you are practicing, you don't want to be fetching balls every minute or two. When you are playing with a bunch of pickleball balls, it's convenient to have a ball hopper to collect them and carry them to and from the court. Hoppers and caddies vary based on their durability and ball capacity. Bigger can be better, but you'll be sacrificing portability. Find a happy medium that works for you.

The Layout of Pickleball Courts

No matter which paddle and ball you choose, the rules, the court, and the etiquette will be the same from game to game. Pickleball is played on a badminton-sized court (20' × 44'), but it can be played indoors or outdoors and as a singles or doubles sport.

Court Layout

Each court has baselines, sidelines, a net, and what's called a kitchen. The kitchen is the rectangular area on either side of the net, also called the Non-Volley Zone, or NVZ. The kitchen prevents players from standing close to the net and hitting a volley (or hitting overheads—also known as overhead slams or smashes—from close range) right at their opponents. It provides a little space from the opponents on each side of the court.

The transition zone (shown in light green in the following figure) refers to part of the court area a few feet inside the baseline and the non-volley line. It is not an official area of the court, but it is meant to reference the area in which players typically hit volleys and half-volleys because of their position on the court.

Indoor versus Outdoor Courts

Similar to tennis, pickleball can be played on either indoor or outdoor courts. While the rules are the same, each setting has its own challenges and specifics (different balls, for example).

Indoor pickleball courts are great because they're not impacted by the weather (strong winds, rain, heat, etc.), so your playing experience will be more consistent. However, the playing surface on indoor courts might not provide consistent playability since the space is often shared with other sports (basketball and volleyball, for example). In addition, the acoustics are often not ideal. If the weather is nice, outdoor courts are a great option. But in bad weather (especially wind and heat), the experience will probably not be as enjoyable. A windy day in particular can wreak havoc with your game.

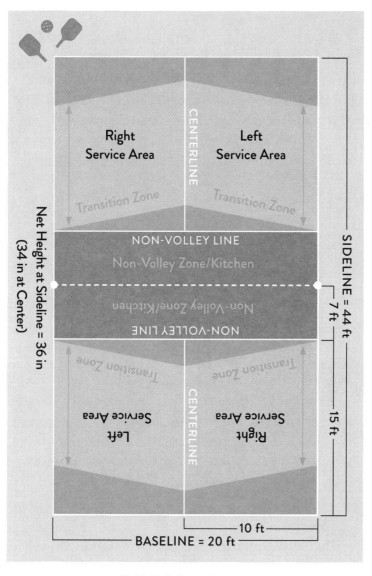

Pickleball Court Layout

Singles versus Doubles

You can also choose between playing singles or doubles. The court size and arrangement are the same for both options. Doubles matches are best for those who prefer to have a designated partner, appreciate teamwork, or don't want the more comprehensive court coverage required in singles play.

DIY Pickleball Court

If you don't have access to dedicated pickleball courts, you can always make your own. At a minimum, you'll want to get a temporary net and some tape (or chalk) to mark the boundaries of the court.

Pickleball Rules

What exactly are the rules of pickleball? Well, there is an entire handbook on the subject—and since rules are added and changed periodically, look for the latest rules at USAPickleball.org. To get started, though, you really just need to know the most important things, which we'll outline in this section. You'll learn how to score your matches, the ins and outs of serving, and a few additional rules to keep in mind.

Scoring

The overall objective of pickleball is to score more points than your opponent until one side reaches 11 and leads by at least 2 points.

Only the server can score points. The player who starts serving continues to do so until they make a fault.

Announcing the Score

Before each serve, the score must be declared out loud, stating the serving team's score first. For doubles matches, both players on a team have a chance to serve. The order of players is also indicated aloud. For example, if the serving team is winning 6 to 2 and the server is the second server, the server would call "6 – 2 – 2."

Serving Rules

There are several rules regarding the mechanics of serving, but once you've served correctly a couple of times, it will become second nature. The basic requirements of serving are as follows:

- Both feet must be behind the baseline prior to starting the serve.
- The server's arm must be moving in an upward arc when it strikes the ball. The serve can be a forehand or backhand style, but it must be performed underhanded.
- The "head" of the paddle must be below the server's wrist when the paddle makes contact with the ball.
- Contact with the ball cannot be made above the waist.
- The server cannot bounce the ball first and then serve off the bounce.

- The serve must be directed to the service area diagonally across from the server.
- When the receiving team wins the serve, the player in the right-hand section of the court starts to play.
- Each player on a team continues to serve until their team makes a fault. The right to serve then passes to the opposing team, which is known as a side out.
- A serve that is not touched by the opponent, resulting in a point for the server/serving team, is called an ace.
- The server will continue to serve until they (or their partner) commit a fault (such as hitting into the net on a serve). The server will also lose their serve if the opposing team hits a winner.

What about Faults and Out-of-Bounds Shots?

At the beginning of a new game, the team serving first is allowed just one fault before handing the ball over to their opponents. After that, players are allowed only one serve, and the ball must clear the 7-foot Non-Volley Zone. The ball is considered "in" if it hits on a centerline, sideline, or baseline (just not the non-volley line).

If the ball is hit out of the court, into the net, or volleyed while in the Non-Volley Zone (including on the non-volley line), this results in a side out, and the other team begins serving. However, if the ball hits the net but lands in the appropriate service court, the server maintains the serve.

After you've got a handle on the basics of serving, you might start experimenting with different kinds of serves, such as high-lob serves, sharp-angled serves, and serves with heavy spin (like topspin).

Other Important Rules and Terms

Here are a few more important rules and terms to know:

- **The difference between a groundstroke and a volley:** A groundstroke is a hit made after the ball bounces off the ground. A volley is a ball hit straight out of the air before having a chance to bounce.
- **The two-bounce rule:** After serving, a ball must be hit via a groundstroke twice before a volley can be attempted—once on the receiver's side and once on the server's side. This gives the receiving team the advantage (at least by position on the court) at the start of each point.
- **"Kitchen" rules:** Pickleball rules are very specific about this space, and it's really what makes pickleball unique from many other paddle and racquet sports. You cannot volley a ball while in the kitchen. As a result, if you hit a ball "shallow" in the kitchen (closer to the net), your opponents can't attack you (that's why this kind of hit is often called an "unattackable" ball). You are giving yourself time to recover and get into a position to respond to the ball that comes back to you. You can step into the kitchen to hit a ball as long as it has bounced first. You just can't be in

the kitchen (this includes any part of your body/clothing) and hit a volley.

What Is a Dink?

A dink is a type of pickleball shot that is hit gently to arc over the net and land within the opponent's NVZ (the closer to the net, the better). To try hitting a dink, meet the ball using a gentle upward motion on your paddle.

Warm-Ups and Cooldowns

Now that you know the rules and have the right equipment, you're almost ready to get out there and play. There is just one more thing to learn about: how to prepare and recover physically. Just like in any sport, stretching and warming up properly before each match and taking care of your body afterward are important aspects of a successful pickleball experience. Paying attention to your conditioning and strength is another key component.

Improve Your Conditioning and Flexibility

Spending time on your flexibility, mobility, strength, and endurance can really pay off in your games. Even casual players can participate in basic exercises that will win them points in the long run. One of the most popular ways to improve your strength and flexibility for pickleball is doing yoga. Cross-training—for example, performing several different types of exercise like jogging, cycling, or strength training—is the most ideal way to condition your body for the sport.

Warm-Up Exercises

Warming up and stretching are essential steps to having an injury-free practice session or match. Try completing a dynamic warm-up (a warm-up consisting of continuous movement) that prepares your body for a rise in internal temperature and physical activity. Exercises with gentle movements—such as lunges, hip and core swings, arm circles, and so on—will help prepare your body for play.

Cooldown Stretches

When it comes to cooling down after practice or matches, static stretching (with no movement) is the way to go. Static stretching after exercise can help you stay limber and promote blood flow, which makes for a quicker and less painful return to the court. Be sure to stretch your key muscles, including hamstrings, quads, shoulders, and triceps.

Rest Up!

When engaging in physical activity like an energetic game of pickleball, your body will need extra time to recover. Ensure that you can sleep for eight to ten hours the night after your game, especially if it is your first time exercising or playing a sport for a while.

Final Thoughts

Congratulations—you now know the basics of pickleball and are ready to take your first steps to becoming a successful player. All that is left is to get out onto a court with a friend and start playing!

MATCH
RECORDS

In this section, you can use the following journal pages to record the scores and conditions of your matches and rate your performance and technical skills on a scale of 1–5. Then take a few moments to reflect on:

- **The court:** Were there any divots in the surface? Was sun glare an issue? Mark any notable issues with the court in the illustration.
- **Match highlights:** Which shots worked well? Be sure to celebrate any impressive points.
- **Match challenges:** Which type of shots tripped you up? Write down any potential areas for improvement.

Finally, jot down the cooldown exercises you chose to do, and note any injuries or discomfort you experienced before, during, or after the match. Let's hit the court!

MATCH DETAILS

Date: /   /

Start Time:

End Time:

Location:

Weather:

FINAL SCORE

WIN/LOSS

PLAYERS

Team 1:

Team 2:

RATE YOUR SKILLS

OVERALL PERFORMANCE

Mental Game:	1	2	3	4	5
Endurance:	1	2	3	4	5
Mobility:	1	2	3	4	5
Teamwork:	1	2	3	4	5
	LOW				HIGH

TECHNICAL SKILLS

Serving:	1	2	3	4	5
Returns:	1	2	3	4	5
Dinking:	1	2	3	4	5
Volleys:	1	2	3	4	5
Offensive Lobs:	1	2	3	4	5
Defensive Lobs:	1	2	3	4	5
Overheads:	1	2	3	4	5
	LOW				HIGH

COURT NOTES

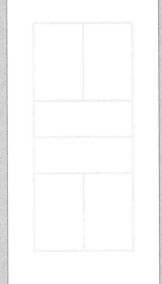

MATCH HIGHLIGHTS

MATCH CHALLENGES

COOLDOWN

INJURIES/DISCOMFORT

MATCH DETAILS

Date: /   /

Start Time: _____

End Time: _____

Location: _____

Weather: _____

FINAL SCORE

WIN/LOSS

PLAYERS

Team 1:

Team 2:

RATE YOUR SKILLS

OVERALL PERFORMANCE

Mental Game:	1	2	3	4	5
Endurance:	1	2	3	4	5
Mobility:	1	2	3	4	5
Teamwork:	1	2	3	4	5

LOW   HIGH

TECHNICAL SKILLS

Serving:	1	2	3	4	5
Returns:	1	2	3	4	5
Dinking:	1	2	3	4	5
Volleys:	1	2	3	4	5
Offensive Lobs:	1	2	3	4	5
Defensive Lobs:	1	2	3	4	5
Overheads:	1	2	3	4	5

LOW   HIGH

COURT NOTES

MATCH HIGHLIGHTS

MATCH CHALLENGES

COOLDOWN

INJURIES/DISCOMFORT

MATCH DETAILS

Date: / /
Start Time: _____
End Time: _____
Location: _____
Weather: _____

FINAL SCORE

WIN/LOSS

PLAYERS

Team 1:

Team 2:

RATE YOUR SKILLS

OVERALL PERFORMANCE

Mental Game:	1	2	3	4	5
Endurance:	1	2	3	4	5
Mobility:	1	2	3	4	5
Teamwork:	1	2	3	4	5

LOW   HIGH

TECHNICAL SKILLS

Serving:	1	2	3	4	5
Returns:	1	2	3	4	5
Dinking:	1	2	3	4	5
Volleys:	1	2	3	4	5
Offensive Lobs:	1	2	3	4	5
Defensive Lobs:	1	2	3	4	5
Overheads:	1	2	3	4	5

LOW   HIGH

COURT NOTES

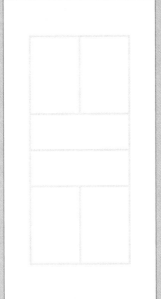

MATCH HIGHLIGHTS

MATCH CHALLENGES

COOLDOWN

INJURIES/DISCOMFORT

MATCH DETAILS

Date: / /
Start Time:
End Time:
Location:
Weather:

FINAL SCORE

WIN/LOSS

PLAYERS

Team 1:

Team 2:

RATE YOUR SKILLS

OVERALL PERFORMANCE

Mental Game:	1	2	3	4	5
Endurance:	1	2	3	4	5
Mobility:	1	2	3	4	5
Teamwork:	1	2	3	4	5

LOW   HIGH

TECHNICAL SKILLS

Serving:	1	2	3	4	5
Returns:	1	2	3	4	5
Dinking:	1	2	3	4	5
Volleys:	1	2	3	4	5
Offensive Lobs:	1	2	3	4	5
Defensive Lobs:	1	2	3	4	5
Overheads:	1	2	3	4	5

LOW   HIGH

COURT NOTES

MATCH HIGHLIGHTS

MATCH CHALLENGES

COOLDOWN

INJURIES/DISCOMFORT

MATCH DETAILS

Date: / /
Start Time:
End Time:
Location:
Weather:

FINAL SCORE

WIN/LOSS

PLAYERS

Team 1:

Team 2:

RATE YOUR SKILLS

OVERALL PERFORMANCE

Mental Game:	1	2	3	4	5
Endurance:	1	2	3	4	5
Mobility:	1	2	3	4	5
Teamwork:	1	2	3	4	5

LOW　　　　　HIGH

TECHNICAL SKILLS

Serving:	1	2	3	4	5
Returns:	1	2	3	4	5
Dinking:	1	2	3	4	5
Volleys:	1	2	3	4	5
Offensive Lobs:	1	2	3	4	5
Defensive Lobs:	1	2	3	4	5
Overheads:	1	2	3	4	5

LOW　　　　　HIGH

COURT NOTES

MATCH HIGHLIGHTS

MATCH CHALLENGES

COOLDOWN

INJURIES/DISCOMFORT

Date: / /

Start Time:

End Time:

Location:

Weather:

WIN/LOSS

Team 1:

Team 2:

OVERALL PERFORMANCE

Mental Game: 1   2   3   4   5

Endurance: 1   2   3   4   5

Mobility: 1   2   3   4   5

Teamwork: 1   2   3   4   5

LOW   HIGH

TECHNICAL SKILLS

Serving: 1   2   3   4   5

Returns: 1   2   3   4   5

Dinking: 1   2   3   4   5

Volleys: 1   2   3   4   5

Offensive Lobs: 1   2   3   4   5

Defensive Lobs: 1   2   3   4   5

Overheads: 1   2   3   4   5

LOW   HIGH

MATCH HIGHLIGHTS

MATCH CHALLENGES

COOLDOWN

INJURIES/DISCOMFORT

Date: / /
Start Time:
End Time:
Location:
Weather:

WIN/LOSS

PLAYERS

Team 1:

Team 2:

RATE YOUR SKILLS

OVERALL PERFORMANCE

Mental Game:	1	2	3	4	5
Endurance:	1	2	3	4	5
Mobility:	1	2	3	4	5
Teamwork:	1	2	3	4	5
	LOW				HIGH

TECHNICAL SKILLS

Serving:	1	2	3	4	5
Returns:	1	2	3	4	5
Dinking:	1	2	3	4	5
Volleys:	1	2	3	4	5
Offensive Lobs:	1	2	3	4	5
Defensive Lobs:	1	2	3	4	5
Overheads:	1	2	3	4	5
	LOW				HIGH

COURT NOTES

MATCH HIGHLIGHTS

MATCH CHALLENGES

COOLDOWN

INJURIES/DISCOMFORT

MATCH DETAILS

Date: / /

Start Time: _____

End Time: _____

Location: _____

Weather: _____

FINAL SCORE

WIN/LOSS

PLAYERS

Team 1:

Team 2:

RATE YOUR SKILLS

OVERALL PERFORMANCE

Mental Game:	1	2	3	4	5
Endurance:	1	2	3	4	5
Mobility:	1	2	3	4	5
Teamwork:	1	2	3	4	5
	LOW				HIGH

TECHNICAL SKILLS

Serving:	1	2	3	4	5
Returns:	1	2	3	4	5
Dinking:	1	2	3	4	5
Volleys:	1	2	3	4	5
Offensive Lobs:	1	2	3	4	5
Defensive Lobs:	1	2	3	4	5
Overheads:	1	2	3	4	5
	LOW				HIGH

COURT NOTES

MATCH HIGHLIGHTS

MATCH CHALLENGES

COOLDOWN

INJURIES/DISCOMFORT

Date: / /
Start Time: _____
End Time: _____
Location: _____
Weather: _____

WIN/LOSS

PLAYERS

Team 1:

Team 2:

RATE YOUR SKILLS

OVERALL PERFORMANCE

Mental Game: 1   2   3   4   5
Endurance: 1   2   3   4   5
Mobility: 1   2   3   4   5
Teamwork: 1   2   3   4   5
                 LOW   HIGH

TECHNICAL SKILLS

Serving: 1   2   3   4   5
Returns: 1   2   3   4   5
Dinking: 1   2   3   4   5
Volleys: 1   2   3   4   5
Offensive Lobs: 1   2   3   4   5
Defensive Lobs: 1   2   3   4   5
Overheads: 1   2   3   4   5
                 LOW   HIGH

COURT NOTES

MATCH HIGHLIGHTS

MATCH CHALLENGES

COOLDOWN

INJURIES/DISCOMFORT

MATCH DETAILS

Date: /   /

Start Time: _____

End Time: _____

Location: _____

Weather: _____

FINAL SCORE

WIN/LOSS

PLAYERS

Team 1:

Team 2:

RATE YOUR SKILLS

OVERALL PERFORMANCE

Mental Game: 1   2   3   4   5

Endurance: 1   2   3   4   5

Mobility: 1   2   3   4   5

Teamwork: 1   2   3   4   5

      LOW   HIGH

TECHNICAL SKILLS

Serving: 1   2   3   4   5

Returns: 1   2   3   4   5

Dinking: 1   2   3   4   5

Volleys: 1   2   3   4   5

Offensive Lobs: 1   2   3   4   5

Defensive Lobs: 1   2   3   4   5

Overheads: 1   2   3   4   5

      LOW   HIGH

COURT NOTES

MATCH HIGHLIGHTS

MATCH CHALLENGES

COOLDOWN

INJURIES/DISCOMFORT

MATCH DETAILS

Date: / /
Start Time:
End Time:
Location:
Weather:

FINAL SCORE

WIN/LOSS

PLAYERS

Team 1:

Team 2:

RATE YOUR SKILLS

OVERALL PERFORMANCE

Mental Game:	1	2	3	4	5
Endurance:	1	2	3	4	5
Mobility:	1	2	3	4	5
Teamwork:	1	2	3	4	5
	LOW				HIGH

TECHNICAL SKILLS

Serving:	1	2	3	4	5
Returns:	1	2	3	4	5
Dinking:	1	2	3	4	5
Volleys:	1	2	3	4	5
Offensive Lobs:	1	2	3	4	5
Defensive Lobs:	1	2	3	4	5
Overheads:	1	2	3	4	5
	LOW				HIGH

COURT NOTES

MATCH HIGHLIGHTS

MATCH CHALLENGES

COOLDOWN

INJURIES/DISCOMFORT

Date: / /
Start Time:
End Time:
Location:
Weather:

FINAL SCORE

WIN/LOSS

PLAYERS

Team 1:

Team 2:

RATE YOUR SKILLS

OVERALL PERFORMANCE

Mental Game:	1	2	3	4	5
Endurance:	1	2	3	4	5
Mobility:	1	2	3	4	5
Teamwork:	1	2	3	4	5
	LOW				HIGH

TECHNICAL SKILLS

Serving:	1	2	3	4	5
Returns:	1	2	3	4	5
Dinking:	1	2	3	4	5
Volleys:	1	2	3	4	5
Offensive Lobs:	1	2	3	4	5
Defensive Lobs:	1	2	3	4	5
Overheads:	1	2	3	4	5
	LOW				HIGH

COURT NOTES

MATCH HIGHLIGHTS

MATCH CHALLENGES

COOLDOWN

INJURIES/DISCOMFORT

MATCH DETAILS

Date: / /
Start Time:
End Time:
Location:
Weather:

FINAL SCORE

WIN/LOSS

PLAYERS

Team 1:

Team 2:

RATE YOUR SKILLS

OVERALL PERFORMANCE

Mental Game: 1 2 3 4 5
Endurance: 1 2 3 4 5
Mobility: 1 2 3 4 5
Teamwork: 1 2 3 4 5

LOW   HIGH

TECHNICAL SKILLS

Serving: 1 2 3 4 5
Returns: 1 2 3 4 5
Dinking: 1 2 3 4 5
Volleys: 1 2 3 4 5
Offensive Lobs: 1 2 3 4 5
Defensive Lobs: 1 2 3 4 5
Overheads: 1 2 3 4 5

LOW   HIGH

COURT NOTES

MATCH HIGHLIGHTS

MATCH CHALLENGES

COOLDOWN

INJURIES/DISCOMFORT

MATCH DETAILS

Date: /   /

Start Time: _____

End Time: _____

Location: _____

Weather: _____

FINAL SCORE

WIN/LOSS

PLAYERS

Team 1:

Team 2:

RATE YOUR SKILLS

OVERALL PERFORMANCE

Mental Game:	1	2	3	4	5
Endurance:	1	2	3	4	5
Mobility:	1	2	3	4	5
Teamwork:	1	2	3	4	5
	LOW				HIGH

TECHNICAL SKILLS

Serving:	1	2	3	4	5
Returns:	1	2	3	4	5
Dinking:	1	2	3	4	5
Volleys:	1	2	3	4	5
Offensive Lobs:	1	2	3	4	5
Defensive Lobs:	1	2	3	4	5
Overheads:	1	2	3	4	5
	LOW				HIGH

COURT NOTES

MATCH HIGHLIGHTS

MATCH CHALLENGES

COOLDOWN

INJURIES/DISCOMFORT

Date: / /
Start Time:
End Time:
Location:
Weather:

FINAL SCORE

WIN/LOSS

PLAYERS

Team 1:

Team 2:

RATE YOUR SKILLS

OVERALL PERFORMANCE

Mental Game:	1	2	3	4	5
Endurance:	1	2	3	4	5
Mobility:	1	2	3	4	5
Teamwork:	1	2	3	4	5
	LOW				HIGH

TECHNICAL SKILLS

Serving:	1	2	3	4	5
Returns:	1	2	3	4	5
Dinking:	1	2	3	4	5
Volleys:	1	2	3	4	5
Offensive Lobs:	1	2	3	4	5
Defensive Lobs:	1	2	3	4	5
Overheads:	1	2	3	4	5
	LOW				HIGH

COURT NOTES

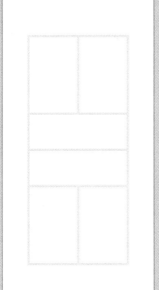

MATCH HIGHLIGHTS

MATCH CHALLENGES

COOLDOWN

INJURIES/DISCOMFORT

MATCH DETAILS

Date: / /
Start Time:
End Time:
Location:
Weather:

FINAL SCORE

WIN/LOSS

PLAYERS

Team 1:   Team 2:

RATE YOUR SKILLS

OVERALL PERFORMANCE

Mental Game: 1 2 3 4 5
Endurance: 1 2 3 4 5
Mobility: 1 2 3 4 5
Teamwork: 1 2 3 4 5
LOW   HIGH

TECHNICAL SKILLS

Serving: 1 2 3 4 5
Returns: 1 2 3 4 5
Dinking: 1 2 3 4 5
Volleys: 1 2 3 4 5
Offensive Lobs: 1 2 3 4 5
Defensive Lobs: 1 2 3 4 5
Overheads: 1 2 3 4 5
LOW   HIGH

COURT NOTES

MATCH HIGHLIGHTS

MATCH CHALLENGES

COOLDOWN

INJURIES/DISCOMFORT

MATCH DETAILS

Date: / /
Start Time:
End Time:
Location:
Weather:

FINAL SCORE

WIN/LOSS

PLAYERS

Team 1:

Team 2:

RATE YOUR SKILLS

OVERALL PERFORMANCE

Mental Game:	1	2	3	4	5
Endurance:	1	2	3	4	5
Mobility:	1	2	3	4	5
Teamwork:	1	2	3	4	5
	LOW				HIGH

TECHNICAL SKILLS

Serving:	1	2	3	4	5
Returns:	1	2	3	4	5
Dinking:	1	2	3	4	5
Volleys:	1	2	3	4	5
Offensive Lobs:	1	2	3	4	5
Defensive Lobs:	1	2	3	4	5
Overheads:	1	2	3	4	5
	LOW				HIGH

COURT NOTES

MATCH HIGHLIGHTS

MATCH CHALLENGES

COOLDOWN

INJURIES/DISCOMFORT

MATCH DETAILS

Date: / /
Start Time: _____
End Time: _____
Location: _____
Weather: _____

FINAL SCORE

WIN/LOSS

PLAYERS

Team 1:

Team 2:

RATE YOUR SKILLS

OVERALL PERFORMANCE

Mental Game: 1   2   3   4   5
Endurance: 1   2   3   4   5
Mobility: 1   2   3   4   5
Teamwork: 1   2   3   4   5
               LOW   HIGH

TECHNICAL SKILLS

Serving: 1   2   3   4   5
Returns: 1   2   3   4   5
Dinking: 1   2   3   4   5
Volleys: 1   2   3   4   5
Offensive Lobs: 1   2   3   4   5
Defensive Lobs: 1   2   3   4   5
Overheads: 1   2   3   4   5
                LOW   HIGH

COURT NOTES

MATCH HIGHLIGHTS

MATCH CHALLENGES

COOLDOWN

INJURIES/DISCOMFORT

MATCH DETAILS

Date: / /
Start Time:
End Time:
Location:
Weather:

FINAL SCORE

WIN/LOSS

PLAYERS

Team 1:

Team 2:

RATE YOUR SKILLS

OVERALL PERFORMANCE

Mental Game: 1 2 3 4 5
Endurance: 1 2 3 4 5
Mobility: 1 2 3 4 5
Teamwork: 1 2 3 4 5
                LOW   HIGH

TECHNICAL SKILLS

Serving: 1 2 3 4 5
Returns: 1 2 3 4 5
Dinking: 1 2 3 4 5
Volleys: 1 2 3 4 5
Offensive Lobs: 1 2 3 4 5
Defensive Lobs: 1 2 3 4 5
Overheads: 1 2 3 4 5
                LOW   HIGH

COURT NOTES

MATCH HIGHLIGHTS

MATCH CHALLENGES

COOLDOWN

INJURIES/DISCOMFORT

MATCH DETAILS

Date: / /
Start Time:
End Time:
Location:
Weather:

FINAL SCORE

WIN/LOSS

PLAYERS

Team 1:

Team 2:

RATE YOUR SKILLS

OVERALL PERFORMANCE

Mental Game: 1 2 3 4 5
Endurance: 1 2 3 4 5
Mobility: 1 2 3 4 5
Teamwork: 1 2 3 4 5
LOW HIGH

TECHNICAL SKILLS

Serving: 1 2 3 4 5
Returns: 1 2 3 4 5
Dinking: 1 2 3 4 5
Volleys: 1 2 3 4 5
Offensive Lobs: 1 2 3 4 5
Defensive Lobs: 1 2 3 4 5
Overheads: 1 2 3 4 5
LOW HIGH

COURT NOTES

MATCH HIGHLIGHTS

MATCH CHALLENGES

COOLDOWN

INJURIES/DISCOMFORT

MATCH DETAILS

Date: / /
Start Time: _____
End Time: _____
Location: _____
Weather: _____

FINAL SCORE

WIN/LOSS

PLAYERS

Team 1:

Team 2:

RATE YOUR SKILLS

OVERALL PERFORMANCE

Mental Game:	1	2	3	4	5
Endurance:	1	2	3	4	5
Mobility:	1	2	3	4	5
Teamwork:	1	2	3	4	5
	LOW				HIGH

TECHNICAL SKILLS

Serving:	1	2	3	4	5
Returns:	1	2	3	4	5
Dinking:	1	2	3	4	5
Volleys:	1	2	3	4	5
Offensive Lobs:	1	2	3	4	5
Defensive Lobs:	1	2	3	4	5
Overheads:	1	2	3	4	5
	LOW				HIGH

COURT NOTES

MATCH HIGHLIGHTS

MATCH CHALLENGES

COOLDOWN

INJURIES/DISCOMFORT

Date: / /
Start Time:
End Time:
Location:
Weather:

WIN/LOSS

PLAYERS

Team 1:

Team 2:

RATE YOUR SKILLS

OVERALL PERFORMANCE

Mental Game:	1	2	3	4	5
Endurance:	1	2	3	4	5
Mobility:	1	2	3	4	5
Teamwork:	1	2	3	4	5
	LOW				HIGH

TECHNICAL SKILLS

Serving:	1	2	3	4	5
Returns:	1	2	3	4	5
Dinking:	1	2	3	4	5
Volleys:	1	2	3	4	5
Offensive Lobs:	1	2	3	4	5
Defensive Lobs:	1	2	3	4	5
Overheads:	1	2	3	4	5
	LOW				HIGH

COURT NOTES

MATCH HIGHLIGHTS

MATCH CHALLENGES

COOLDOWN

INJURIES/DISCOMFORT

MATCH DETAILS

Date: / /
Start Time:
End Time:
Location:
Weather:

FINAL SCORE

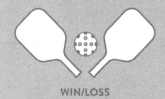

WIN/LOSS

PLAYERS

Team 1:

Team 2:

RATE YOUR SKILLS

OVERALL PERFORMANCE

Mental Game: 1 2 3 4 5
Endurance: 1 2 3 4 5
Mobility: 1 2 3 4 5
Teamwork: 1 2 3 4 5
LOW   HIGH

TECHNICAL SKILLS

Serving: 1 2 3 4 5
Returns: 1 2 3 4 5
Dinking: 1 2 3 4 5
Volleys: 1 2 3 4 5
Offensive Lobs: 1 2 3 4 5
Defensive Lobs: 1 2 3 4 5
Overheads: 1 2 3 4 5
LOW   HIGH

COURT NOTES

MATCH HIGHLIGHTS

MATCH CHALLENGES

COOLDOWN

INJURIES/DISCOMFORT

MATCH DETAILS

Date: / /
Start Time:
End Time:
Location:
Weather:

FINAL SCORE

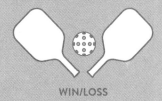

WIN/LOSS

PLAYERS

Team 1:

Team 2:

RATE YOUR SKILLS

OVERALL PERFORMANCE

Mental Game:	1	2	3	4	5
Endurance:	1	2	3	4	5
Mobility:	1	2	3	4	5
Teamwork:	1	2	3	4	5
	LOW				HIGH

TECHNICAL SKILLS

Serving:	1	2	3	4	5
Returns:	1	2	3	4	5
Dinking:	1	2	3	4	5
Volleys:	1	2	3	4	5
Offensive Lobs:	1	2	3	4	5
Defensive Lobs:	1	2	3	4	5
Overheads:	1	2	3	4	5
	LOW				HIGH

COURT NOTES

MATCH HIGHLIGHTS

MATCH CHALLENGES

COOLDOWN

INJURIES/DISCOMFORT

Date: / /

Start Time:

End Time:

Location:

Weather:

WIN/LOSS

PLAYERS

Team 1:

Team 2:

RATE YOUR SKILLS

OVERALL PERFORMANCE

Mental Game:	1	2	3	4	5
Endurance:	1	2	3	4	5
Mobility:	1	2	3	4	5
Teamwork:	1	2	3	4	5
	LOW				HIGH

TECHNICAL SKILLS

Serving:	1	2	3	4	5
Returns:	1	2	3	4	5
Dinking:	1	2	3	4	5
Volleys:	1	2	3	4	5
Offensive Lobs:	1	2	3	4	5
Defensive Lobs:	1	2	3	4	5
Overheads:	1	2	3	4	5
	LOW				HIGH

COURT NOTES

MATCH HIGHLIGHTS

MATCH CHALLENGES

COOLDOWN

INJURIES/DISCOMFORT

MATCH DETAILS

Date: / /
Start Time: _____
End Time: _____
Location: _____
Weather: _____

FINAL SCORE

WIN/LOSS

PLAYERS

Team 1:

Team 2:

RATE YOUR SKILLS

OVERALL PERFORMANCE

Mental Game:	1	2	3	4	5
Endurance:	1	2	3	4	5
Mobility:	1	2	3	4	5
Teamwork:	1	2	3	4	5
	LOW				HIGH

TECHNICAL SKILLS

Serving:	1	2	3	4	5
Returns:	1	2	3	4	5
Dinking:	1	2	3	4	5
Volleys:	1	2	3	4	5
Offensive Lobs:	1	2	3	4	5
Defensive Lobs:	1	2	3	4	5
Overheads:	1	2	3	4	5
	LOW				HIGH

COURT NOTES

MATCH HIGHLIGHTS

MATCH CHALLENGES

COOLDOWN

INJURIES/DISCOMFORT

Date: / /

Start Time:

End Time:

Location:

Weather:

WIN/LOSS

PLAYERS

Team 1:

Team 2:

RATE YOUR SKILLS

OVERALL PERFORMANCE

Mental Game:	1	2	3	4	5
Endurance:	1	2	3	4	5
Mobility:	1	2	3	4	5
Teamwork:	1	2	3	4	5
	LOW				HIGH

TECHNICAL SKILLS

Serving:	1	2	3	4	5
Returns:	1	2	3	4	5
Dinking:	1	2	3	4	5
Volleys:	1	2	3	4	5
Offensive Lobs:	1	2	3	4	5
Defensive Lobs:	1	2	3	4	5
Overheads:	1	2	3	4	5
	LOW				HIGH

COURT NOTES

MATCH HIGHLIGHTS

MATCH CHALLENGES

COOLDOWN

INJURIES/DISCOMFORT

Date: / /
Start Time:
End Time:
Location:
Weather:

WIN/LOSS

Team 1: Team 2:

OVERALL PERFORMANCE

Mental Game:	1	2	3	4	5
Endurance:	1	2	3	4	5
Mobility:	1	2	3	4	5
Teamwork:	1	2	3	4	5
	LOW				HIGH

TECHNICAL SKILLS

Serving:	1	2	3	4	5
Returns:	1	2	3	4	5
Dinking:	1	2	3	4	5
Volleys:	1	2	3	4	5
Offensive Lobs:	1	2	3	4	5
Defensive Lobs:	1	2	3	4	5
Overheads:	1	2	3	4	5
	LOW				HIGH

MATCH HIGHLIGHTS

MATCH CHALLENGES

COOLDOWN

INJURIES/DISCOMFORT

MATCH DETAILS

Date: / /
Start Time:
End Time:
Location:
Weather:

FINAL SCORE

WIN/LOSS

PLAYERS

Team 1:

Team 2:

RATE YOUR SKILLS

OVERALL PERFORMANCE

Mental Game:	1	2	3	4	5
Endurance:	1	2	3	4	5
Mobility:	1	2	3	4	5
Teamwork:	1	2	3	4	5
	LOW				HIGH

TECHNICAL SKILLS

Serving:	1	2	3	4	5
Returns:	1	2	3	4	5
Dinking:	1	2	3	4	5
Volleys:	1	2	3	4	5
Offensive Lobs:	1	2	3	4	5
Defensive Lobs:	1	2	3	4	5
Overheads:	1	2	3	4	5
	LOW				HIGH

COURT NOTES

MATCH HIGHLIGHTS

MATCH CHALLENGES

COOLDOWN

INJURIES/DISCOMFORT

MATCH DETAILS

Date: / /

Start Time:

End Time:

Location:

Weather:

FINAL SCORE

WIN/LOSS

PLAYERS

Team 1:

Team 2:

RATE YOUR SKILLS

OVERALL PERFORMANCE

Mental Game:	1	2	3	4	5
Endurance:	1	2	3	4	5
Mobility:	1	2	3	4	5
Teamwork:	1	2	3	4	5
	LOW				HIGH

TECHNICAL SKILLS

Serving:	1	2	3	4	5
Returns:	1	2	3	4	5
Dinking:	1	2	3	4	5
Volleys:	1	2	3	4	5
Offensive Lobs:	1	2	3	4	5
Defensive Lobs:	1	2	3	4	5
Overheads:	1	2	3	4	5
	LOW				HIGH

COURT NOTES

MATCH HIGHLIGHTS

MATCH CHALLENGES

COOLDOWN

INJURIES/DISCOMFORT

MATCH DETAILS

Date: / /
Start Time:
End Time:
Location:
Weather:

FINAL SCORE

WIN/LOSS

PLAYERS

Team 1:

Team 2:

RATE YOUR SKILLS

OVERALL PERFORMANCE

Mental Game:	1	2	3	4	5
Endurance:	1	2	3	4	5
Mobility:	1	2	3	4	5
Teamwork:	1	2	3	4	5
	LOW				HIGH

TECHNICAL SKILLS

Serving:	1	2	3	4	5
Returns:	1	2	3	4	5
Dinking:	1	2	3	4	5
Volleys:	1	2	3	4	5
Offensive Lobs:	1	2	3	4	5
Defensive Lobs:	1	2	3	4	5
Overheads:	1	2	3	4	5
	LOW				HIGH

COURT NOTES

MATCH HIGHLIGHTS

MATCH CHALLENGES

COOLDOWN

INJURIES/DISCOMFORT

MATCH DETAILS

Date: /   /

Start Time: _____

End Time: _____

Location: _____

Weather: _____

FINAL SCORE

WIN/LOSS

PLAYERS

Team 1:

Team 2:

RATE YOUR SKILLS

OVERALL PERFORMANCE

Mental Game: 1   2   3   4   5

Endurance: 1   2   3   4   5

Mobility: 1   2   3   4   5

Teamwork: 1   2   3   4   5

         LOW   HIGH

TECHNICAL SKILLS

Serving: 1   2   3   4   5

Returns: 1   2   3   4   5

Dinking: 1   2   3   4   5

Volleys: 1   2   3   4   5

Offensive Lobs: 1   2   3   4   5

Defensive Lobs: 1   2   3   4   5

Overheads: 1   2   3   4   5

         LOW   HIGH

COURT NOTES

MATCH HIGHLIGHTS

MATCH CHALLENGES

COOLDOWN

INJURIES/DISCOMFORT

MATCH DETAILS

Date: / /

Start Time:

End Time:

Location:

Weather:

FINAL SCORE

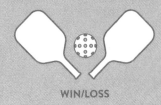

WIN/LOSS

PLAYERS

Team 1:

Team 2:

RATE YOUR SKILLS

OVERALL PERFORMANCE

Mental Game:	1	2	3	4	5
Endurance:	1	2	3	4	5
Mobility:	1	2	3	4	5
Teamwork:	1	2	3	4	5
	LOW				HIGH

TECHNICAL SKILLS

Serving:	1	2	3	4	5
Returns:	1	2	3	4	5
Dinking:	1	2	3	4	5
Volleys:	1	2	3	4	5
Offensive Lobs:	1	2	3	4	5
Defensive Lobs:	1	2	3	4	5
Overheads:	1	2	3	4	5
	LOW				HIGH

COURT NOTES

MATCH HIGHLIGHTS

MATCH CHALLENGES

COOLDOWN

INJURIES/DISCOMFORT

MATCH DETAILS

Date: / /
Start Time:
End Time:
Location:
Weather:

FINAL SCORE

WIN/LOSS

PLAYERS

Team 1:

Team 2:

RATE YOUR SKILLS

OVERALL PERFORMANCE

Mental Game:	1	2	3	4	5
Endurance:	1	2	3	4	5
Mobility:	1	2	3	4	5
Teamwork:	1	2	3	4	5
	LOW				HIGH

TECHNICAL SKILLS

Serving:	1	2	3	4	5
Returns:	1	2	3	4	5
Dinking:	1	2	3	4	5
Volleys:	1	2	3	4	5
Offensive Lobs:	1	2	3	4	5
Defensive Lobs:	1	2	3	4	5
Overheads:	1	2	3	4	5
	LOW				HIGH

COURT NOTES

MATCH HIGHLIGHTS

MATCH CHALLENGES

COOLDOWN

INJURIES/DISCOMFORT

MATCH DETAILS

Date: /   /

Start Time: _____

End Time: _____

Location: _____

Weather: _____

FINAL SCORE

WIN/LOSS

PLAYERS

Team 1:

Team 2:

RATE YOUR SKILLS

OVERALL PERFORMANCE

Mental Game:	1	2	3	4	5
Endurance:	1	2	3	4	5
Mobility:	1	2	3	4	5
Teamwork:	1	2	3	4	5
	LOW				HIGH

TECHNICAL SKILLS

Serving:	1	2	3	4	5
Returns:	1	2	3	4	5
Dinking:	1	2	3	4	5
Volleys:	1	2	3	4	5
Offensive Lobs:	1	2	3	4	5
Defensive Lobs:	1	2	3	4	5
Overheads:	1	2	3	4	5
	LOW				HIGH

COURT NOTES

MATCH HIGHLIGHTS

MATCH CHALLENGES

COOLDOWN

INJURIES/DISCOMFORT

MATCH DETAILS

Date: / /

Start Time:

End Time:

Location:

Weather:

FINAL SCORE

WIN/LOSS

PLAYERS

Team 1:

Team 2:

RATE YOUR SKILLS

OVERALL PERFORMANCE

Mental Game:	1	2	3	4	5
Endurance:	1	2	3	4	5
Mobility:	1	2	3	4	5
Teamwork:	1	2	3	4	5

LOW   HIGH

TECHNICAL SKILLS

Serving:	1	2	3	4	5
Returns:	1	2	3	4	5
Dinking:	1	2	3	4	5
Volleys:	1	2	3	4	5
Offensive Lobs:	1	2	3	4	5
Defensive Lobs:	1	2	3	4	5
Overheads:	1	2	3	4	5

LOW   HIGH

COURT NOTES

MATCH HIGHLIGHTS

MATCH CHALLENGES

COOLDOWN

INJURIES/DISCOMFORT

MATCH DETAILS

Date: /   /

Start Time:

End Time:

Location:

Weather:

FINAL SCORE

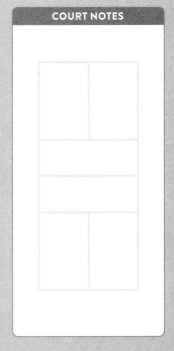

WIN/LOSS

PLAYERS

Team 1:

Team 2:

RATE YOUR SKILLS

OVERALL PERFORMANCE

Mental Game: 1   2   3   4   5

Endurance: 1   2   3   4   5

Mobility: 1   2   3   4   5

Teamwork: 1   2   3   4   5

LOW   HIGH

TECHNICAL SKILLS

Serving: 1   2   3   4   5

Returns: 1   2   3   4   5

Dinking: 1   2   3   4   5

Volleys: 1   2   3   4   5

Offensive Lobs: 1   2   3   4   5

Defensive Lobs: 1   2   3   4   5

Overheads: 1   2   3   4   5

LOW   HIGH

COURT NOTES

MATCH HIGHLIGHTS

MATCH CHALLENGES

COOLDOWN

INJURIES/DISCOMFORT

MATCH DETAILS

Date: / /

Start Time: _____

End Time: _____

Location: _____

Weather: _____

FINAL SCORE

WIN/LOSS

PLAYERS

Team 1:

Team 2:

RATE YOUR SKILLS

OVERALL PERFORMANCE

Mental Game:	1	2	3	4	5
Endurance:	1	2	3	4	5
Mobility:	1	2	3	4	5
Teamwork:	1	2	3	4	5

LOW   HIGH

TECHNICAL SKILLS

Serving:	1	2	3	4	5
Returns:	1	2	3	4	5
Dinking:	1	2	3	4	5
Volleys:	1	2	3	4	5
Offensive Lobs:	1	2	3	4	5
Defensive Lobs:	1	2	3	4	5
Overheads:	1	2	3	4	5

LOW   HIGH

COURT NOTES

MATCH HIGHLIGHTS

MATCH CHALLENGES

COOLDOWN

INJURIES/DISCOMFORT

MATCH DETAILS

Date: / /
Start Time: _____
End Time: _____
Location: _____
Weather: _____

FINAL SCORE

WIN/LOSS

PLAYERS

Team 1:

Team 2:

RATE YOUR SKILLS

OVERALL PERFORMANCE

Mental Game: 1   2   3   4   5
Endurance: 1   2   3   4   5
Mobility: 1   2   3   4   5
Teamwork: 1   2   3   4   5
               LOW   HIGH

TECHNICAL SKILLS

Serving: 1   2   3   4   5
Returns: 1   2   3   4   5
Dinking: 1   2   3   4   5
Volleys: 1   2   3   4   5
Offensive Lobs: 1   2   3   4   5
Defensive Lobs: 1   2   3   4   5
Overheads: 1   2   3   4   5
                LOW   HIGH

COURT NOTES

MATCH HIGHLIGHTS

MATCH CHALLENGES

COOLDOWN

INJURIES/DISCOMFORT

MATCH DETAILS

Date: / /
Start Time:
End Time:
Location:
Weather:

FINAL SCORE

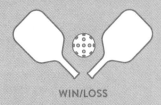

WIN/LOSS

PLAYERS

Team 1:

Team 2:

RATE YOUR SKILLS

OVERALL PERFORMANCE

Mental Game:	1	2	3	4	5
Endurance:	1	2	3	4	5
Mobility:	1	2	3	4	5
Teamwork:	1	2	3	4	5
	LOW				HIGH

TECHNICAL SKILLS

Serving:	1	2	3	4	5
Returns:	1	2	3	4	5
Dinking:	1	2	3	4	5
Volleys:	1	2	3	4	5
Offensive Lobs:	1	2	3	4	5
Defensive Lobs:	1	2	3	4	5
Overheads:	1	2	3	4	5
	LOW				HIGH

COURT NOTES

MATCH HIGHLIGHTS

MATCH CHALLENGES

COOLDOWN

INJURIES/DISCOMFORT

MATCH DETAILS

Date: /   /
Start Time:
End Time:
Location:
Weather:

FINAL SCORE

WIN/LOSS

PLAYERS

Team 1:

Team 2:

RATE YOUR SKILLS

OVERALL PERFORMANCE

Mental Game:	1	2	3	4	5
Endurance:	1	2	3	4	5
Mobility:	1	2	3	4	5
Teamwork:	1	2	3	4	5

LOW   HIGH

TECHNICAL SKILLS

Serving:	1	2	3	4	5
Returns:	1	2	3	4	5
Dinking:	1	2	3	4	5
Volleys:	1	2	3	4	5
Offensive Lobs:	1	2	3	4	5
Defensive Lobs:	1	2	3	4	5
Overheads:	1	2	3	4	5

LOW   HIGH

COURT NOTES

MATCH HIGHLIGHTS

MATCH CHALLENGES

COOLDOWN

INJURIES/DISCOMFORT

MATCH DETAILS

Date: / /
Start Time:
End Time:
Location:
Weather:

FINAL SCORE

WIN/LOSS

PLAYERS

Team 1:

Team 2:

RATE YOUR SKILLS

OVERALL PERFORMANCE

Mental Game:	1	2	3	4	5
Endurance:	1	2	3	4	5
Mobility:	1	2	3	4	5
Teamwork:	1	2	3	4	5
	LOW				HIGH

TECHNICAL SKILLS

Serving:	1	2	3	4	5
Returns:	1	2	3	4	5
Dinking:	1	2	3	4	5
Volleys:	1	2	3	4	5
Offensive Lobs:	1	2	3	4	5
Defensive Lobs:	1	2	3	4	5
Overheads:	1	2	3	4	5
	LOW				HIGH

COURT NOTES

MATCH HIGHLIGHTS

MATCH CHALLENGES

COOLDOWN

INJURIES/DISCOMFORT

Date: / /
Start Time: _____
End Time: _____
Location: _____
Weather: _____

FINAL SCORE

WIN/LOSS

PLAYERS

Team 1:

Team 2:

RATE YOUR SKILLS

OVERALL PERFORMANCE

Mental Game:	1	2	3	4	5
Endurance:	1	2	3	4	5
Mobility:	1	2	3	4	5
Teamwork:	1	2	3	4	5
	LOW				HIGH

TECHNICAL SKILLS

Serving:	1	2	3	4	5
Returns:	1	2	3	4	5
Dinking:	1	2	3	4	5
Volleys:	1	2	3	4	5
Offensive Lobs:	1	2	3	4	5
Defensive Lobs:	1	2	3	4	5
Overheads:	1	2	3	4	5
	LOW				HIGH

COURT NOTES

MATCH HIGHLIGHTS

MATCH CHALLENGES

COOLDOWN

INJURIES/DISCOMFORT

Date: / /

Start Time:

End Time:

Location:

Weather:

FINAL SCORE

WIN/LOSS

PLAYERS

Team 1:

Team 2:

RATE YOUR SKILLS

OVERALL PERFORMANCE

Mental Game:	1	2	3	4	5
Endurance:	1	2	3	4	5
Mobility:	1	2	3	4	5
Teamwork:	1	2	3	4	5
	LOW				HIGH

TECHNICAL SKILLS

Serving:	1	2	3	4	5
Returns:	1	2	3	4	5
Dinking:	1	2	3	4	5
Volleys:	1	2	3	4	5
Offensive Lobs:	1	2	3	4	5
Defensive Lobs:	1	2	3	4	5
Overheads:	1	2	3	4	5
	LOW				HIGH

COURT NOTES

MATCH HIGHLIGHTS

MATCH CHALLENGES

COOLDOWN

INJURIES/DISCOMFORT

MATCH DETAILS

Date: / /

Start Time:

End Time:

Location:

Weather:

FINAL SCORE

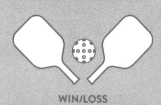

WIN/LOSS

PLAYERS

Team 1:

Team 2:

RATE YOUR SKILLS

OVERALL PERFORMANCE

Mental Game: 1   2   3   4   5

Endurance: 1   2   3   4   5

Mobility: 1   2   3   4   5

Teamwork: 1   2   3   4   5

LOW   HIGH

TECHNICAL SKILLS

Serving: 1   2   3   4   5

Returns: 1   2   3   4   5

Dinking: 1   2   3   4   5

Volleys: 1   2   3   4   5

Offensive Lobs: 1   2   3   4   5

Defensive Lobs: 1   2   3   4   5

Overheads: 1   2   3   4   5

LOW   HIGH

COURT NOTES

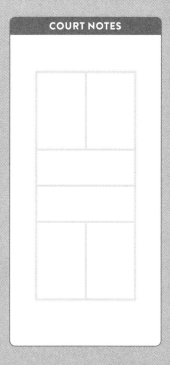

MATCH HIGHLIGHTS

MATCH CHALLENGES

COOLDOWN

INJURIES/DISCOMFORT

MATCH DETAILS

Date: / /
Start Time:
End Time:
Location:
Weather:

FINAL SCORE

WIN/LOSS

PLAYERS

Team 1:

Team 2:

RATE YOUR SKILLS

OVERALL PERFORMANCE

Mental Game:	1	2	3	4	5
Endurance:	1	2	3	4	5
Mobility:	1	2	3	4	5
Teamwork:	1	2	3	4	5
	LOW				HIGH

TECHNICAL SKILLS

Serving:	1	2	3	4	5
Returns:	1	2	3	4	5
Dinking:	1	2	3	4	5
Volleys:	1	2	3	4	5
Offensive Lobs:	1	2	3	4	5
Defensive Lobs:	1	2	3	4	5
Overheads:	1	2	3	4	5
	LOW				HIGH

COURT NOTES

MATCH HIGHLIGHTS

MATCH CHALLENGES

COOLDOWN

INJURIES/DISCOMFORT

MATCH DETAILS

Date: / /

Start Time:

End Time:

Location:

Weather:

FINAL SCORE

WIN/LOSS

PLAYERS

Team 1:

Team 2:

RATE YOUR SKILLS

OVERALL PERFORMANCE

Mental Game:	1	2	3	4	5
Endurance:	1	2	3	4	5
Mobility:	1	2	3	4	5
Teamwork:	1	2	3	4	5

LOW   HIGH

TECHNICAL SKILLS

Serving:	1	2	3	4	5
Returns:	1	2	3	4	5
Dinking:	1	2	3	4	5
Volleys:	1	2	3	4	5
Offensive Lobs:	1	2	3	4	5
Defensive Lobs:	1	2	3	4	5
Overheads:	1	2	3	4	5

LOW   HIGH

COURT NOTES

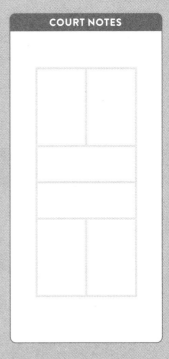

MATCH HIGHLIGHTS

MATCH CHALLENGES

COOLDOWN

INJURIES/DISCOMFORT

MATCH DETAILS

Date: / /

Start Time:

End Time:

Location:

Weather:

FINAL SCORE

WIN/LOSS

PLAYERS

Team 1:

Team 2:

RATE YOUR SKILLS

OVERALL PERFORMANCE

Mental Game:	1	2	3	4	5
Endurance:	1	2	3	4	5
Mobility:	1	2	3	4	5
Teamwork:	1	2	3	4	5

LOW   HIGH

TECHNICAL SKILLS

Serving:	1	2	3	4	5
Returns:	1	2	3	4	5
Dinking:	1	2	3	4	5
Volleys:	1	2	3	4	5
Offensive Lobs:	1	2	3	4	5
Defensive Lobs:	1	2	3	4	5
Overheads:	1	2	3	4	5

LOW   HIGH

COURT NOTES

MATCH HIGHLIGHTS

MATCH CHALLENGES

COOLDOWN

INJURIES/DISCOMFORT

MATCH DETAILS

Date: / /
Start Time:
End Time:
Location:
Weather:

FINAL SCORE

WIN/LOSS

PLAYERS

Team 1:

Team 2:

RATE YOUR SKILLS

OVERALL PERFORMANCE

Mental Game: 1 2 3 4 5
Endurance: 1 2 3 4 5
Mobility: 1 2 3 4 5
Teamwork: 1 2 3 4 5
                 LOW   HIGH

TECHNICAL SKILLS

Serving: 1 2 3 4 5
Returns: 1 2 3 4 5
Dinking: 1 2 3 4 5
Volleys: 1 2 3 4 5
Offensive Lobs: 1 2 3 4 5
Defensive Lobs: 1 2 3 4 5
Overheads: 1 2 3 4 5
                 LOW   HIGH

COURT NOTES

MATCH HIGHLIGHTS

MATCH CHALLENGES

COOLDOWN

INJURIES/DISCOMFORT

MATCH DETAILS

Date: / /
Start Time:
End Time:
Location:
Weather:

FINAL SCORE

WIN/LOSS

PLAYERS

Team 1:

Team 2:

RATE YOUR SKILLS

OVERALL PERFORMANCE

Mental Game:	1	2	3	4	5
Endurance:	1	2	3	4	5
Mobility:	1	2	3	4	5
Teamwork:	1	2	3	4	5
	LOW				HIGH

TECHNICAL SKILLS

Serving:	1	2	3	4	5
Returns:	1	2	3	4	5
Dinking:	1	2	3	4	5
Volleys:	1	2	3	4	5
Offensive Lobs:	1	2	3	4	5
Defensive Lobs:	1	2	3	4	5
Overheads:	1	2	3	4	5
	LOW				HIGH

COURT NOTES

MATCH HIGHLIGHTS

MATCH CHALLENGES

COOLDOWN

INJURIES/DISCOMFORT

MATCH DETAILS

Date: / /
Start Time:
End Time:
Location:
Weather:

FINAL SCORE

WIN/LOSS

PLAYERS

Team 1:

Team 2:

RATE YOUR SKILLS

OVERALL PERFORMANCE

Mental Game: 1   2   3   4   5
Endurance: 1   2   3   4   5
Mobility: 1   2   3   4   5
Teamwork: 1   2   3   4   5
               LOW   HIGH

TECHNICAL SKILLS

Serving: 1   2   3   4   5
Returns: 1   2   3   4   5
Dinking: 1   2   3   4   5
Volleys: 1   2   3   4   5
Offensive Lobs: 1   2   3   4   5
Defensive Lobs: 1   2   3   4   5
Overheads: 1   2   3   4   5
                 LOW   HIGH

COURT NOTES

MATCH HIGHLIGHTS

MATCH CHALLENGES

COOLDOWN

INJURIES/DISCOMFORT

MATCH DETAILS

Date: / /
Start Time:
End Time:
Location:
Weather:

FINAL SCORE

WIN/LOSS

PLAYERS

Team 1:

Team 2:

RATE YOUR SKILLS

OVERALL PERFORMANCE

Mental Game:	1	2	3	4	5
Endurance:	1	2	3	4	5
Mobility:	1	2	3	4	5
Teamwork:	1	2	3	4	5
	LOW				HIGH

TECHNICAL SKILLS

Serving:	1	2	3	4	5
Returns:	1	2	3	4	5
Dinking:	1	2	3	4	5
Volleys:	1	2	3	4	5
Offensive Lobs:	1	2	3	4	5
Defensive Lobs:	1	2	3	4	5
Overheads:	1	2	3	4	5
	LOW				HIGH

COURT NOTES

MATCH HIGHLIGHTS

MATCH CHALLENGES

COOLDOWN

INJURIES/DISCOMFORT

Date: / /

Start Time:

End Time:

Location:

Weather:

WIN/LOSS

Team 1:

Team 2:

OVERALL PERFORMANCE

Mental Game:	1	2	3	4	5
Endurance:	1	2	3	4	5
Mobility:	1	2	3	4	5
Teamwork:	1	2	3	4	5
	LOW				HIGH

TECHNICAL SKILLS

Serving:	1	2	3	4	5
Returns:	1	2	3	4	5
Dinking:	1	2	3	4	5
Volleys:	1	2	3	4	5
Offensive Lobs:	1	2	3	4	5
Defensive Lobs:	1	2	3	4	5
Overheads:	1	2	3	4	5
	LOW				HIGH

MATCH HIGHLIGHTS

MATCH CHALLENGES

COOLDOWN

INJURIES/DISCOMFORT

MATCH DETAILS

Date: /   /

Start Time:

End Time:

Location:

Weather:

FINAL SCORE

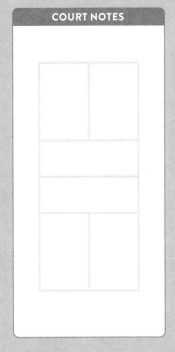

WIN/LOSS

PLAYERS

Team 1:

Team 2:

RATE YOUR SKILLS

OVERALL PERFORMANCE

Mental Game:	1	2	3	4	5
Endurance:	1	2	3	4	5
Mobility:	1	2	3	4	5
Teamwork:	1	2	3	4	5
	LOW				HIGH

TECHNICAL SKILLS

Serving:	1	2	3	4	5
Returns:	1	2	3	4	5
Dinking:	1	2	3	4	5
Volleys:	1	2	3	4	5
Offensive Lobs:	1	2	3	4	5
Defensive Lobs:	1	2	3	4	5
Overheads:	1	2	3	4	5
	LOW				HIGH

COURT NOTES

MATCH HIGHLIGHTS

MATCH CHALLENGES

COOLDOWN

INJURIES/DISCOMFORT

MATCH DETAILS

Date: / /
Start Time:
End Time:
Location:
Weather:

FINAL SCORE

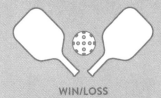

WIN/LOSS

PLAYERS

Team 1:

Team 2:

RATE YOUR SKILLS

OVERALL PERFORMANCE

Mental Game:	1	2	3	4	5
Endurance:	1	2	3	4	5
Mobility:	1	2	3	4	5
Teamwork:	1	2	3	4	5
	LOW				HIGH

TECHNICAL SKILLS

Serving:	1	2	3	4	5
Returns:	1	2	3	4	5
Dinking:	1	2	3	4	5
Volleys:	1	2	3	4	5
Offensive Lobs:	1	2	3	4	5
Defensive Lobs:	1	2	3	4	5
Overheads:	1	2	3	4	5
	LOW				HIGH

COURT NOTES

MATCH HIGHLIGHTS

MATCH CHALLENGES

COOLDOWN

INJURIES/DISCOMFORT

MATCH DETAILS

Date: / /

Start Time: _____

End Time: _____

Location: _____

Weather: _____

FINAL SCORE

WIN/LOSS

PLAYERS

Team 1:

Team 2:

RATE YOUR SKILLS

OVERALL PERFORMANCE

Mental Game:	1	2	3	4	5
Endurance:	1	2	3	4	5
Mobility:	1	2	3	4	5
Teamwork:	1	2	3	4	5

LOW   HIGH

TECHNICAL SKILLS

Serving:	1	2	3	4	5
Returns:	1	2	3	4	5
Dinking:	1	2	3	4	5
Volleys:	1	2	3	4	5
Offensive Lobs:	1	2	3	4	5
Defensive Lobs:	1	2	3	4	5
Overheads:	1	2	3	4	5

LOW   HIGH

COURT NOTES

MATCH HIGHLIGHTS

MATCH CHALLENGES

COOLDOWN

INJURIES/DISCOMFORT

MATCH DETAILS

Date: /   /
Start Time: _____
End Time: _____
Location: _____
Weather: _____

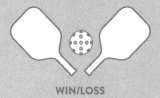

WIN/LOSS

PLAYERS

Team 1:

Team 2:

RATE YOUR SKILLS

OVERALL PERFORMANCE

Mental Game: 1 2 3 4 5
Endurance: 1 2 3 4 5
Mobility: 1 2 3 4 5
Teamwork: 1 2 3 4 5
               LOW   HIGH

TECHNICAL SKILLS

Serving: 1 2 3 4 5
Returns: 1 2 3 4 5
Dinking: 1 2 3 4 5
Volleys: 1 2 3 4 5
Offensive Lobs: 1 2 3 4 5
Defensive Lobs: 1 2 3 4 5
Overheads: 1 2 3 4 5
                LOW   HIGH

COURT NOTES

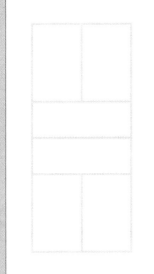

MATCH HIGHLIGHTS

MATCH CHALLENGES

COOLDOWN

INJURIES/DISCOMFORT

Date: / /
Start Time:
End Time:
Location:
Weather:

WIN/LOSS

PLAYERS

Team 1:

Team 2:

RATE YOUR SKILLS

OVERALL PERFORMANCE

Mental Game:	1	2	3	4	5
Endurance:	1	2	3	4	5
Mobility:	1	2	3	4	5
Teamwork:	1	2	3	4	5
	LOW				HIGH

TECHNICAL SKILLS

Serving:	1	2	3	4	5
Returns:	1	2	3	4	5
Dinking:	1	2	3	4	5
Volleys:	1	2	3	4	5
Offensive Lobs:	1	2	3	4	5
Defensive Lobs:	1	2	3	4	5
Overheads:	1	2	3	4	5
	LOW				HIGH

COURT NOTES

MATCH HIGHLIGHTS

MATCH CHALLENGES

COOLDOWN

INJURIES/DISCOMFORT

MATCH DETAILS

Date: / /
Start Time:
End Time:
Location:
Weather:

FINAL SCORE

WIN/LOSS

PLAYERS

Team 1:

Team 2:

RATE YOUR SKILLS

OVERALL PERFORMANCE

Mental Game:	1	2	3	4	5
Endurance:	1	2	3	4	5
Mobility:	1	2	3	4	5
Teamwork:	1	2	3	4	5
	LOW				HIGH

TECHNICAL SKILLS

Serving:	1	2	3	4	5
Returns:	1	2	3	4	5
Dinking:	1	2	3	4	5
Volleys:	1	2	3	4	5
Offensive Lobs:	1	2	3	4	5
Defensive Lobs:	1	2	3	4	5
Overheads:	1	2	3	4	5
	LOW				HIGH

COURT NOTES

MATCH HIGHLIGHTS

MATCH CHALLENGES

COOLDOWN

INJURIES/DISCOMFORT

MATCH DETAILS

Date: /   /

Start Time: _____

End Time: _____

Location: _____

Weather: _____

FINAL SCORE

WIN/LOSS

PLAYERS

Team 1:

Team 2:

RATE YOUR SKILLS

OVERALL PERFORMANCE

Mental Game:	1	2	3	4	5
Endurance:	1	2	3	4	5
Mobility:	1	2	3	4	5
Teamwork:	1	2	3	4	5
	LOW				HIGH

TECHNICAL SKILLS

Serving:	1	2	3	4	5
Returns:	1	2	3	4	5
Dinking:	1	2	3	4	5
Volleys:	1	2	3	4	5
Offensive Lobs:	1	2	3	4	5
Defensive Lobs:	1	2	3	4	5
Overheads:	1	2	3	4	5
	LOW				HIGH

COURT NOTES

MATCH HIGHLIGHTS

MATCH CHALLENGES

COOLDOWN

INJURIES/DISCOMFORT

MATCH DETAILS

Date: / /

Start Time: _____

End Time: _____

Location: _____

Weather: _____

FINAL SCORE

WIN/LOSS

PLAYERS

Team 1:

Team 2:

RATE YOUR SKILLS

OVERALL PERFORMANCE

Mental Game:	1	2	3	4	5
Endurance:	1	2	3	4	5
Mobility:	1	2	3	4	5
Teamwork:	1	2	3	4	5
	LOW				HIGH

TECHNICAL SKILLS

Serving:	1	2	3	4	5
Returns:	1	2	3	4	5
Dinking:	1	2	3	4	5
Volleys:	1	2	3	4	5
Offensive Lobs:	1	2	3	4	5
Defensive Lobs:	1	2	3	4	5
Overheads:	1	2	3	4	5
	LOW				HIGH

COURT NOTES

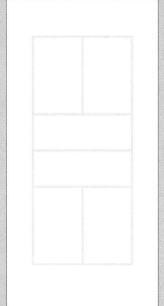

MATCH HIGHLIGHTS

MATCH CHALLENGES

COOLDOWN

INJURIES/DISCOMFORT

MATCH DETAILS

Date: /   /

Start Time: _____

End Time: _____

Location: _____

Weather: _____

FINAL SCORE

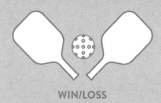

WIN/LOSS

PLAYERS

Team 1:

Team 2:

RATE YOUR SKILLS

OVERALL PERFORMANCE

Mental Game: 1   2   3   4   5

Endurance: 1   2   3   4   5

Mobility: 1   2   3   4   5

Teamwork: 1   2   3   4   5

      LOW   HIGH

TECHNICAL SKILLS

Serving: 1   2   3   4   5

Returns: 1   2   3   4   5

Dinking: 1   2   3   4   5

Volleys: 1   2   3   4   5

Offensive Lobs: 1   2   3   4   5

Defensive Lobs: 1   2   3   4   5

Overheads: 1   2   3   4   5

      LOW   HIGH

COURT NOTES

MATCH HIGHLIGHTS

MATCH CHALLENGES

COOLDOWN

INJURIES/DISCOMFORT

MATCH DETAILS

Date: / /
Start Time: _____
End Time: _____
Location: _____
Weather: _____

FINAL SCORE

WIN/LOSS

PLAYERS

Team 1:

Team 2:

RATE YOUR SKILLS

OVERALL PERFORMANCE

Mental Game:	1	2	3	4	5
Endurance:	1	2	3	4	5
Mobility:	1	2	3	4	5
Teamwork:	1	2	3	4	5
	LOW				HIGH

TECHNICAL SKILLS

Serving:	1	2	3	4	5
Returns:	1	2	3	4	5
Dinking:	1	2	3	4	5
Volleys:	1	2	3	4	5
Offensive Lobs:	1	2	3	4	5
Defensive Lobs:	1	2	3	4	5
Overheads:	1	2	3	4	5
	LOW				HIGH

COURT NOTES

MATCH HIGHLIGHTS

MATCH CHALLENGES

COOLDOWN

INJURIES/DISCOMFORT

MATCH DETAILS

Date: / /

Start Time: _____

End Time: _____

Location: _____

Weather: _____

FINAL SCORE

WIN/LOSS

PLAYERS

Team 1:

Team 2:

RATE YOUR SKILLS

OVERALL PERFORMANCE

Mental Game:	1	2	3	4	5
Endurance:	1	2	3	4	5
Mobility:	1	2	3	4	5
Teamwork:	1	2	3	4	5
	LOW				HIGH

TECHNICAL SKILLS

Serving:	1	2	3	4	5
Returns:	1	2	3	4	5
Dinking:	1	2	3	4	5
Volleys:	1	2	3	4	5
Offensive Lobs:	1	2	3	4	5
Defensive Lobs:	1	2	3	4	5
Overheads:	1	2	3	4	5
	LOW				HIGH

COURT NOTES

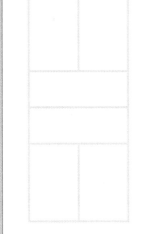

MATCH HIGHLIGHTS

MATCH CHALLENGES

COOLDOWN

INJURIES/DISCOMFORT

MATCH DETAILS

Date: /   /

Start Time:

End Time:

Location:

Weather:

FINAL SCORE

WIN/LOSS

PLAYERS

Team 1:

Team 2:

RATE YOUR SKILLS

OVERALL PERFORMANCE

Mental Game: 1   2   3   4   5

Endurance: 1   2   3   4   5

Mobility: 1   2   3   4   5

Teamwork: 1   2   3   4   5

LOW   HIGH

TECHNICAL SKILLS

Serving: 1   2   3   4   5

Returns: 1   2   3   4   5

Dinking: 1   2   3   4   5

Volleys: 1   2   3   4   5

Offensive Lobs: 1   2   3   4   5

Defensive Lobs: 1   2   3   4   5

Overheads: 1   2   3   4   5

LOW   HIGH

COURT NOTES

MATCH HIGHLIGHTS

MATCH CHALLENGES

COOLDOWN

INJURIES/DISCOMFORT

MATCH DETAILS

Date: / /
Start Time:
End Time:
Location:
Weather:

FINAL SCORE

WIN/LOSS

PLAYERS

Team 1:

Team 2:

RATE YOUR SKILLS

OVERALL PERFORMANCE

Mental Game:	1	2	3	4	5
Endurance:	1	2	3	4	5
Mobility:	1	2	3	4	5
Teamwork:	1	2	3	4	5
	LOW				HIGH

TECHNICAL SKILLS

Serving:	1	2	3	4	5
Returns:	1	2	3	4	5
Dinking:	1	2	3	4	5
Volleys:	1	2	3	4	5
Offensive Lobs:	1	2	3	4	5
Defensive Lobs:	1	2	3	4	5
Overheads:	1	2	3	4	5
	LOW				HIGH

COURT NOTES

MATCH HIGHLIGHTS

MATCH CHALLENGES

COOLDOWN

INJURIES/DISCOMFORT

MATCH DETAILS

Date: / /
Start Time:
End Time:
Location:
Weather:

FINAL SCORE

WIN/LOSS

PLAYERS

Team 1:

Team 2:

RATE YOUR SKILLS

OVERALL PERFORMANCE

Mental Game:	1	2	3	4	5
Endurance:	1	2	3	4	5
Mobility:	1	2	3	4	5
Teamwork:	1	2	3	4	5
	LOW				HIGH

TECHNICAL SKILLS

Serving:	1	2	3	4	5
Returns:	1	2	3	4	5
Dinking:	1	2	3	4	5
Volleys:	1	2	3	4	5
Offensive Lobs:	1	2	3	4	5
Defensive Lobs:	1	2	3	4	5
Overheads:	1	2	3	4	5
	LOW				HIGH

COURT NOTES

MATCH HIGHLIGHTS

MATCH CHALLENGES

COOLDOWN

INJURIES/DISCOMFORT

MATCH DETAILS

Date: / /

Start Time:

End Time:

Location:

Weather:

FINAL SCORE

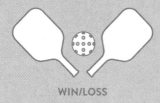

WIN/LOSS

PLAYERS

Team 1:

Team 2:

RATE YOUR SKILLS

OVERALL PERFORMANCE

Mental Game:	1	2	3	4	5
Endurance:	1	2	3	4	5
Mobility:	1	2	3	4	5
Teamwork:	1	2	3	4	5
	LOW				HIGH

TECHNICAL SKILLS

Serving:	1	2	3	4	5
Returns:	1	2	3	4	5
Dinking:	1	2	3	4	5
Volleys:	1	2	3	4	5
Offensive Lobs:	1	2	3	4	5
Defensive Lobs:	1	2	3	4	5
Overheads:	1	2	3	4	5
	LOW				HIGH

COURT NOTES

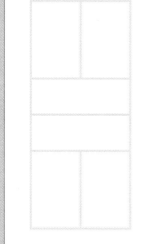

MATCH HIGHLIGHTS

MATCH CHALLENGES

COOLDOWN

INJURIES/DISCOMFORT

MATCH DETAILS

Date: /   /

Start Time: _____

End Time: _____

Location: _____

Weather: _____

FINAL SCORE

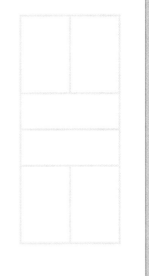

WIN/LOSS

PLAYERS

Team 1:

Team 2:

RATE YOUR SKILLS

OVERALL PERFORMANCE

Mental Game:	1	2	3	4	5
Endurance:	1	2	3	4	5
Mobility:	1	2	3	4	5
Teamwork:	1	2	3	4	5
	LOW				HIGH

TECHNICAL SKILLS

Serving:	1	2	3	4	5
Returns:	1	2	3	4	5
Dinking:	1	2	3	4	5
Volleys:	1	2	3	4	5
Offensive Lobs:	1	2	3	4	5
Defensive Lobs:	1	2	3	4	5
Overheads:	1	2	3	4	5
	LOW				HIGH

COURT NOTES

MATCH HIGHLIGHTS

MATCH CHALLENGES

COOLDOWN

INJURIES/DISCOMFORT

MATCH DETAILS

Date: /   /

Start Time: _____

End Time: _____

Location: _____

Weather: _____

FINAL SCORE

WIN/LOSS

PLAYERS

Team 1:

Team 2:

RATE YOUR SKILLS

OVERALL PERFORMANCE

Mental Game:	1	2	3	4	5
Endurance:	1	2	3	4	5
Mobility:	1	2	3	4	5
Teamwork:	1	2	3	4	5
	LOW				HIGH

TECHNICAL SKILLS

Serving:	1	2	3	4	5
Returns:	1	2	3	4	5
Dinking:	1	2	3	4	5
Volleys:	1	2	3	4	5
Offensive Lobs:	1	2	3	4	5
Defensive Lobs:	1	2	3	4	5
Overheads:	1	2	3	4	5
	LOW				HIGH

COURT NOTES

MATCH HIGHLIGHTS

MATCH CHALLENGES

COOLDOWN

INJURIES/DISCOMFORT

MATCH DETAILS

Date: / /
Start Time: _____
End Time: _____
Location: _____
Weather: _____

FINAL SCORE

WIN/LOSS

PLAYERS

Team 1: | Team 2:

RATE YOUR SKILLS

OVERALL PERFORMANCE

Mental Game: 1 2 3 4 5
Endurance: 1 2 3 4 5
Mobility: 1 2 3 4 5
Teamwork: 1 2 3 4 5
              LOW   HIGH

TECHNICAL SKILLS

Serving: 1 2 3 4 5
Returns: 1 2 3 4 5
Dinking: 1 2 3 4 5
Volleys: 1 2 3 4 5
Offensive Lobs: 1 2 3 4 5
Defensive Lobs: 1 2 3 4 5
Overheads: 1 2 3 4 5
                LOW   HIGH

COURT NOTES

MATCH HIGHLIGHTS

MATCH CHALLENGES

COOLDOWN

INJURIES/DISCOMFORT

MATCH DETAILS

Date: /   /

Start Time: _____

End Time: _____

Location: _____

Weather: _____

FINAL SCORE

WIN/LOSS

PLAYERS

Team 1:

Team 2:

RATE YOUR SKILLS

OVERALL PERFORMANCE

Mental Game: 1   2   3   4   5

Endurance: 1   2   3   4   5

Mobility: 1   2   3   4   5

Teamwork: 1   2   3   4   5

LOW   HIGH

TECHNICAL SKILLS

Serving: 1   2   3   4   5

Returns: 1   2   3   4   5

Dinking: 1   2   3   4   5

Volleys: 1   2   3   4   5

Offensive Lobs: 1   2   3   4   5

Defensive Lobs: 1   2   3   4   5

Overheads: 1   2   3   4   5

LOW   HIGH

COURT NOTES

MATCH HIGHLIGHTS

MATCH CHALLENGES

COOLDOWN

INJURIES/DISCOMFORT

MATCH DETAILS

Date: / /
Start Time: _____
End Time: _____
Location: _____
Weather: _____

FINAL SCORE

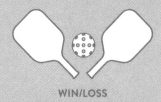

WIN/LOSS

PLAYERS

Team 1:

Team 2:

RATE YOUR SKILLS

OVERALL PERFORMANCE

Mental Game:	1	2	3	4	5
Endurance:	1	2	3	4	5
Mobility:	1	2	3	4	5
Teamwork:	1	2	3	4	5

LOW · HIGH

TECHNICAL SKILLS

Serving:	1	2	3	4	5
Returns:	1	2	3	4	5
Dinking:	1	2	3	4	5
Volleys:	1	2	3	4	5
Offensive Lobs:	1	2	3	4	5
Defensive Lobs:	1	2	3	4	5
Overheads:	1	2	3	4	5

LOW · HIGH

COURT NOTES

MATCH HIGHLIGHTS

MATCH CHALLENGES

COOLDOWN

INJURIES/DISCOMFORT

MATCH DETAILS

Date: / /

Start Time:

End Time:

Location:

Weather:

FINAL SCORE

WIN/LOSS

PLAYERS

Team 1:

Team 2:

RATE YOUR SKILLS

OVERALL PERFORMANCE

Mental Game: 1 2 3 4 5

Endurance: 1 2 3 4 5

Mobility: 1 2 3 4 5

Teamwork: 1 2 3 4 5

LOW   HIGH

TECHNICAL SKILLS

Serving: 1 2 3 4 5

Returns: 1 2 3 4 5

Dinking: 1 2 3 4 5

Volleys: 1 2 3 4 5

Offensive Lobs: 1 2 3 4 5

Defensive Lobs: 1 2 3 4 5

Overheads: 1 2 3 4 5

LOW   HIGH

COURT NOTES

MATCH HIGHLIGHTS

MATCH CHALLENGES

COOLDOWN

INJURIES/DISCOMFORT

MATCH DETAILS

Date: / /
Start Time:
End Time:
Location:
Weather:

FINAL SCORE

WIN/LOSS

PLAYERS

Team 1:   Team 2:

RATE YOUR SKILLS

OVERALL PERFORMANCE

Mental Game: 1 2 3 4 5
Endurance: 1 2 3 4 5
Mobility: 1 2 3 4 5
Teamwork: 1 2 3 4 5
                LOW   HIGH

TECHNICAL SKILLS

Serving: 1 2 3 4 5
Returns: 1 2 3 4 5
Dinking: 1 2 3 4 5
Volleys: 1 2 3 4 5
Offensive Lobs: 1 2 3 4 5
Defensive Lobs: 1 2 3 4 5
Overheads: 1 2 3 4 5
                LOW   HIGH

COURT NOTES

MATCH HIGHLIGHTS

MATCH CHALLENGES

COOLDOWN

INJURIES/DISCOMFORT

MATCH DETAILS

Date: /   /

Start Time: _____

End Time: _____

Location: _____

Weather: _____

FINAL SCORE

WIN/LOSS

PLAYERS

Team 1:

Team 2:

RATE YOUR SKILLS

OVERALL PERFORMANCE

Mental Game: 1   2   3   4   5

Endurance: 1   2   3   4   5

Mobility: 1   2   3   4   5

Teamwork: 1   2   3   4   5

LOW   HIGH

TECHNICAL SKILLS

Serving: 1   2   3   4   5

Returns: 1   2   3   4   5

Dinking: 1   2   3   4   5

Volleys: 1   2   3   4   5

Offensive Lobs: 1   2   3   4   5

Defensive Lobs: 1   2   3   4   5

Overheads: 1   2   3   4   5

LOW   HIGH

COURT NOTES

MATCH HIGHLIGHTS

MATCH CHALLENGES

COOLDOWN

INJURIES/DISCOMFORT

MATCH DETAILS

Date: /   /

Start Time:

End Time:

Location:

Weather:

FINAL SCORE

WIN/LOSS

PLAYERS

Team 1:

Team 2:

RATE YOUR SKILLS

OVERALL PERFORMANCE

Mental Game:	1	2	3	4	5
Endurance:	1	2	3	4	5
Mobility:	1	2	3	4	5
Teamwork:	1	2	3	4	5

LOW   HIGH

TECHNICAL SKILLS

Serving:	1	2	3	4	5
Returns:	1	2	3	4	5
Dinking:	1	2	3	4	5
Volleys:	1	2	3	4	5
Offensive Lobs:	1	2	3	4	5
Defensive Lobs:	1	2	3	4	5
Overheads:	1	2	3	4	5

LOW   HIGH

COURT NOTES

MATCH HIGHLIGHTS

MATCH CHALLENGES

COOLDOWN

INJURIES/DISCOMFORT

MATCH DETAILS

Date: / /

Start Time: _____

End Time: _____

Location: _____

Weather: _____

FINAL SCORE

WIN/LOSS

PLAYERS

Team 1:

Team 2:

RATE YOUR SKILLS

OVERALL PERFORMANCE

Mental Game:	1	2	3	4	5
Endurance:	1	2	3	4	5
Mobility:	1	2	3	4	5
Teamwork:	1	2	3	4	5

LOW   HIGH

TECHNICAL SKILLS

Serving:	1	2	3	4	5
Returns:	1	2	3	4	5
Dinking:	1	2	3	4	5
Volleys:	1	2	3	4	5
Offensive Lobs:	1	2	3	4	5
Defensive Lobs:	1	2	3	4	5
Overheads:	1	2	3	4	5

LOW   HIGH

COURT NOTES

MATCH HIGHLIGHTS

MATCH CHALLENGES

COOLDOWN

INJURIES/DISCOMFORT

MATCH DETAILS

Date: /   /
Start Time:
End Time:
Location:
Weather:

FINAL SCORE

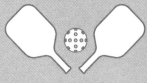

WIN/LOSS

PLAYERS

Team 1:   Team 2:

RATE YOUR SKILLS

OVERALL PERFORMANCE

Mental Game:	1	2	3	4	5
Endurance:	1	2	3	4	5
Mobility:	1	2	3	4	5
Teamwork:	1	2	3	4	5

LOW   HIGH

TECHNICAL SKILLS

Serving:	1	2	3	4	5
Returns:	1	2	3	4	5
Dinking:	1	2	3	4	5
Volleys:	1	2	3	4	5
Offensive Lobs:	1	2	3	4	5
Defensive Lobs:	1	2	3	4	5
Overheads:	1	2	3	4	5

LOW   HIGH

COURT NOTES

MATCH HIGHLIGHTS

MATCH CHALLENGES

COOLDOWN

INJURIES/DISCOMFORT

MATCH DETAILS

Date: /   /

Start Time: _____

End Time: _____

Location: _____

Weather: _____

FINAL SCORE

WIN/LOSS

PLAYERS

Team 1:

Team 2:

RATE YOUR SKILLS

OVERALL PERFORMANCE

Mental Game:	1	2	3	4	5
Endurance:	1	2	3	4	5
Mobility:	1	2	3	4	5
Teamwork:	1	2	3	4	5
	LOW				HIGH

TECHNICAL SKILLS

Serving:	1	2	3	4	5
Returns:	1	2	3	4	5
Dinking:	1	2	3	4	5
Volleys:	1	2	3	4	5
Offensive Lobs:	1	2	3	4	5
Defensive Lobs:	1	2	3	4	5
Overheads:	1	2	3	4	5
	LOW				HIGH

COURT NOTES

MATCH HIGHLIGHTS

MATCH CHALLENGES

COOLDOWN

INJURIES/DISCOMFORT

Glossary

Ace:
A legal serve that lands in the opponent's service box and is not touched by the opponent, resulting in a point for the server/serving team.

Around the Post (ATP):
A shot that is hit off the court, outside of the net post, usually off a wide dink, that lands in the opponents' court.

Backhand:
A shot where a player hits the ball with their paddle using a swinging motion that crosses the body with the back of the hand leading.

Banger:
Slang for a player who often hits shots hard at their opponents even when there are better alternatives. A banger tries to win points with brute force versus strategy and finesse.

Baseline:

The line at the back of the pickleball court that is 22 feet from the net. Balls that bounce beyond here first are out of play.

Centerline:

The line starting at the non-volley line (also known as the kitchen line) and running parallel to the sidelines that evenly separates the service courts.

Dink:

A soft shot that is hit to arc over the net and land within the opponent's kitchen (NVZ).

Fault:

A violation of one of the rules that results in a stoppage of play. Faults can occur during the serve (such as a foot fault) as well as during a rally (such as hitting the ball into the net or out of bounds).

Forehand:

A shot hit with the paddle on the same side as the hand holding it, striking the ball with the palm facing the opposing team.

Game:

A segment of play where players or teams compete to be the first to reach a predetermined number of points, typically 11, while maintaining at least a 2-point lead. Most matches are determined by the first player or team to win two out of three games.

Groundstroke:

A shot where the ball is hit after one bounce.

Half-volley:

A shot where the player hits the ball immediately after it has bounced and before it reaches the maximum height of its bounce.

Kitchen:

Also called the Non-Volley Zone. This is the area of the court marked off 7 feet from the net, and no player may step into this area to hit a ball unless the ball has bounced first.

Lob:

A player hits the ball high in the air (and often deeper into the opposing team's court). Lobs are either offensive (usually hit up at the kitchen line and intended to drive the opponents toward the baseline of their court) or defensive (as a way to buy more time when in trouble).

Match:

A set number of games in a series that determine a winner. The match is often best-of-three or best-of-five games, with each game usually played to 11 (and sometimes 15 or 21) points.

Non-Volley Zone (NVZ):

The area of the court from the net to the line 7 feet from the net, bounded by the two sidelines, the non-volley line, and the net. Also known as the kitchen. A player may not step into this area to hit a ball unless it has first bounced.

Overhead slam/smash:

An aggressive shot that is struck above the player's head that forces the ball quickly downward. This forceful shot can often make it difficult for the opponents to return effectively. It is typically hit as a response to a lob from an opponent.

Paddle:

The flat-faced implement used to strike the pickleball ball. It is comparable to a racquet in tennis or badminton and has a solid surface (typically composite material, carbon, or Nomex) instead of strings, as on a tennis racquet.

Poach:

In doubles play, to cross over into your partner's area to play a ball that was meant for them. This often surprises an opponent by taking time away from them.

Rally:

Ongoing play between opponents that occurs after the serve and before a fault.

Receiver:

This is the player diagonally across from the server who will be returning the ball.

Serve:

The act of putting the pickleball ball into play at the beginning of each point.

Sideline:

The line at the side of the court that designates in and out of bounds.

Side out:

Occurs when the service team commits a fault and subsequently loses their serve. Serving then goes over to the opponents.

Third shot (drop):

The third shot of a point that is hit by the serving team. A drop is designed to bounce in the opponents' kitchen to allow time for the serving team to advance up to their non-volley line. The third shot can also be hit as a drive or as a lob and is often determined based on the return from the opponents.

Transition zone:

Refers to part of the court area a few feet inside the baseline and the non-volley line. It is not an official area of the court, but it is meant to reference the area in between where a player takes groundstrokes (at the back of the court) and where a player hits volleys or dinks. In this zone, players typically hit volleys and half-volleys because of their position on the court.

Two-bounce rule:

This rule states that the receiver must let the serve bounce first before hitting it, and the serving team must let the return bounce before hitting it. No volleys may be hit in either case. After the third shot, the ball may be volleyed by any team.

Volley:

Hitting the ball in the air without letting it bounce first.

Conversion Chart

US Length Measurements	Metric Equivalent
¼ inch	0.6 centimeters
½ inch	1.2 centimeters
¾ inch	1.9 centimeters
1 inch	2.5 centimeters
1½ inches	3.8 centimeters
1 foot	0.3 meters
1 yard	0.9 meters